Renewable Energy

Contents | **Page**

written by John Lockyer

Red Rocket Readers™
Engineered by Flying Start Books

Lights need energy. Cars need energy. The screens we watch need energy, too. Energy is here, there, and everywhere.

city lights

A lot of energy comes from coal, gas, and oil. One day, the coal, gas, and oil will run out.

Now there are more ways to make energy. Energy can come from the wind.

Big fans are set up on cliffs, hills, and in the sea. The fans spin in the wind to make energy.

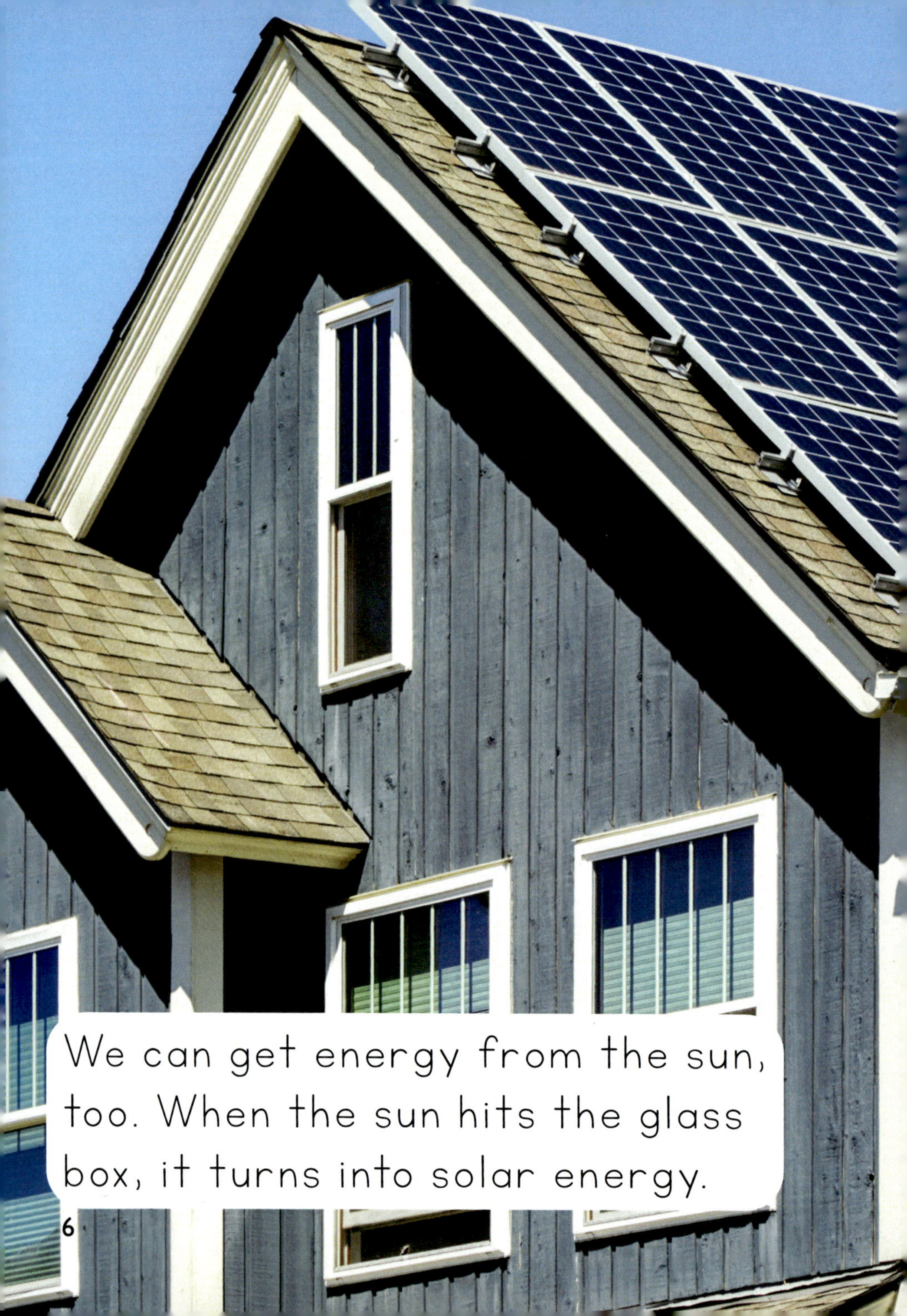

We can get energy from the sun, too. When the sun hits the glass box, it turns into solar energy.

Solar farms are set up where there is lots of sun. The glass boxes track the sun as it shifts in the sky.

There is energy inside the Earth. In some places, there are hot rocks and water under the earth.

The hot rocks and the water make steam. The steam comes up out of the earth in pipes. It spins big fans to make energy.

A dam can make energy from water. Water drops into a gap and then spills down a big pipe.

At the bottom, the water hits a big fan and spins it. As the fan spins, it makes energy.

hydro dam

We can make energy when we burn stuff. Trash is good to burn. This is one of the best ways to get rid of things.

When we burn stuff, we make heat. Then the heat can make energy for big mills.

Most cars and trucks run on gas. Now many cars and trucks run on a battery.

We plug the battery in to get energy. These electric cars and trucks do not make smog.

electric car

Energy that comes from the sun, the wind, water, or a battery will not run out. It is renewable. Renewable energy is best for the planet.